Watch Out for Banana Peels
and Other Important Sesame Safety Tips

By Sarah Albee
Illustrated by Tom Brannon

Published by Dalmatian Press, 2011, an imprint of Dalmatian Publishing Group, Franklin, Tennessee 37067. No part of this book may be reproduced or copied in any form without written permission from the copyright owner. 1-866-418-2572

Printed in China

CE12916/0111/ZHE

SAFETY TIP #2: Clean up toys and spills that could make someone fall. And watch out for banana peels!

Uh-oh.

CAUTION WET FLOOR

SAFETY TIP #4: Never pet a strange dog.